Thoughts

A collection of life ponderings

Maria Collier

Made with ❤ on the BookLeaf Publishing Platform

www.bookleafpub.in

www.bookleafpub.com

Dedication

To my husband who was my rock during the hardest year of our lives.

Preface

From an early age, writing has been my way of making sense of the world around me and the emotions that often felt too overwhelming to name. Poetry, in particular, captured my heart when I discovered how the rhythm and rhyme of words could soothe my soul, especially during the turbulent times at home.

Throughout high school, I found myself drawn to poetry readings, where I marveled at how another person's words could touch me so deeply—how they could make me feel their pain, joy, longing, and hope as though those emotions were my own.

This collection is shaped by a blend of personal experiences, reflections sparked by books I've read, conversations with friends, and moments when writing became a means of moving forward. Each poem is a step along my journey, a way to process and release what I carry inside.

I hope these poems resonate with you, and that you find a connection in the feelings within each line. May they echo your own thoughts, and offer something to hold onto as you read.

Acknowledgements

I am deeply grateful to my parents, whose unwavering support and dedication to the value of learning have shaped who I am today. Your belief in me has been a constant source of strength. To my siblings, thank you for the joy, love, and strength you bring into my life— your presence means the world to me.
A special thank you to my husband, whose faith in me and encouragement to keep creating emboldens my journey.

I am forever thankful to the many teachers who have nurtured my talents and helped me grow into the person and writer I am today. To the many writers and poets who have made my soul soar with their words and inspired me to write my own.

Lastly, I owe everything I have to God, whose grace and guidance continue to lead me forward.

1. Lost

I'm lost ...
I don't know how I got here,
Or why, or when, or where ...

I'm lost ...
  And alone ...
    And wishful ...
      And here - just here
Wanting to scream and kick, and run
Wanting to laugh, and kiss and hug

But I'm just here -
Lonely and lost

2. Knowing

I never knew how much I loved you
   I never knew how much you loved me, too

I never knew
  My heart
Could hurt this much
  Without you
I never knew you knew

And it is in this state of knowing
  That my soul decides to fly
– Crossing mountains and oceans
To take refuge in your arms

3. Survival

I can imagine a life without you
A sky with no stars
A time before language
A primitive age
When survival was the value of the day

I can imagine a world without sound
In which no bells ring
In which birds have gone silent
Across skies muted by lack of sun

What I cannot imagine is my survival
Still living, still breathing,
When it is air that I am missing

I am trying not to miss you
I am trying not to breathe

4. Voice

Today, I heard your voice in my dreams,
    It spoke to me while my soul was asleep
It shook me, and pulled me,
    And it made me land at your feet.
It woke every nerve of my body
    And each fiber of my soul.
Today, I heard your voice in my dreams,
    It spoke to me while my soul was asleep
It made me aware of your being around me
    And it consumed me with longing and drear
It warmed my heart
    It freed my soul
Today, you woke me up
    From a lonely reverie

5. Your

Longing
For the sound
Of your voice
And the
Sparkle of your eyes

Longing
For the roughness
Of your hands
And the warmth
Of your embrace

6. Naked

Naked
Stripped of all my
    Defenses
        Prejudices
            And
                Idiosyncrasies

Naked
As a tree in the dead of winter
With no memory of spring

7. Rights and Desires

I know I have no right to love you
    But I do
I know I shouldn't expect you to write to me
    But when you don't
My heart sinks and the world is duller and emptier until
you do
Then my eyes can't read fast enough
While my heart does misses a beat

I know I shouldn't wish you
Here next to me
But every time the wind brushes my skin
I close my eyes and imagine
Your breath caressing my neck and ears
And wish I was losing myself in your embrace

8. Self-reliant

8

The stillness of the moment
When you realize it's up to you
Nobody is willing to do for you
What you do for others without thought
The noticing, the observing, the doing, the jumping in
It's just you
Sure, others are willing
But even when you ask, it's on their terms and not yours
Be still my heart and beat for you

9. Moments

That moment when you wish
Words spoken would be forgotten
When the only sound you hear
Is your heart shattering
Into slivers that will
Never be put together again

That moment when the one who
Kept you going
Is now the one who makes you wish
For the day's end

That moment when your life seems
To stop but the world keeps turning
And what you know and trust
Is swept from underneath your feet

The moment when you must go on
Because you have to
Because somehow or another
Your heart keeps beating, you
Keep breathing, and the
Sun comes up again

10. The Morning After

It always hits you
The morning after

The sun rises, you open your eyes
And it hits you
The words come back
The sighs, the glances
The unspoken truths
The truths that should have never been spoken

And the tears come back
Though rains flowed out
Yesterday, the dam has been
Opened and the heart won't be quenched

And then, it hits you again
That there's a morning after
That the sun rose again
That your eyes opened
And your body still breathes
And feels

The morning after, and the one after
That, and after one more, and
Then your realize, it hits you no more

11. Break Up

All the plans,
The pinky promises
The unspoken deals
The virtual dates

The future hugs
The longed for kisses
The stolen glances
The smiles to share

The random thoughts
The unexpected texts
The morning emails
The writing rituals

They all counted on forever
They didn't foresee the end

The blank calendar
The broken promises
The forgotten deals
The offline sign

The empty arms
The longing lips
The blank stares
The unseen tears

The sad memories
The quiet phone
The deserted inbox
The unwritten words

12. The Sun's Kiss

It started slow
A single ray gleaming through the clouds
I close my eyes and beg for more

For the warmth to come closer
And touch my nose
For the golden rays to reach my face
Glide over my eyes and make me moan

Lustfully, blissfully, hungrily
I want for the clouds to part
For the skies to clear
And the sun to shine

My heart pounds as the rays come near
And the anticipation grows

And then it's there
Surrounding my all
Parting my lips
Warm, sweet breath,
Infusing life into my soul

The clouds move in
But my eyes smile
As the sun strokes my hair
Promising an encore

13. Grief

Pain knows no boundaries
It comes at you when you
Least expect it
– at the sound of a key
At a glimpse of her photograph
At the sweet smell of her old shawl

It sucker punches you right at the gut
Robbing you of breath
As it makes tears roll down
Your cheeks

The void in your heart expands
And all the carefully
Glued together pieces
Come apart
Reminding you that once
Broken
Your heart will never be intact

14. Shadows

As I look at myself in the mirror
I see only a shadow of myself

The skinny legs
The scarred torso
The thinning hair
The sad eyes

It takes awhile for my
Vision to blur
As the tears come down

But then in that
Blurry, evanescent vision of myself
I find her - I find who
I used to be
And I see that her strength and
Determination are still there

That her kindness hasn't diminished
Just because she went through hell
That her inner joy is waiting
To burst out in a smile
And that love has protected

Her heart from shattering away

'It's just a shadow'
I tell myself in the mirror
But you're still there

15. Perhaps

Perhaps the night won't end
Perhaps the dark will stand
Perhaps I was never meant
To be less than alive

Perhaps the day will come
Perhaps the light will shine
Perhaps the pain will fade
As the sun comes up

16. Happiness

A helping hand

A brand new book

An orange sunset

A lilac sunrise

A mountain hike

An ocean wave

A smiling baby

A quiet hug

An easy day

A yummy meal

A cold glass water on a summer day

A favorite song in the radio

An aromatic bouquet

17. To Be or Not to Be

It is not who we are
It is not who we were
It is who we become
When adversity comes knocking at our door

It is not what we have
What we dream, what we love
It's who stays close to us
When the monsters come for our souls

It is not when we break
When we cry or when we fall
It's who extends a hand
And lifts us off the floor

It is who we are after the darkness has gone
It is what we choose when a new life has begun
It is where we go after facing our demons and thinking
We had nowhere to go

18. Heart to Brain

22

I find a place in my brain
where my emotions fit in while I make sense of them
I catalog them and file them in a way
where I can retrieve them later
A place that's easily accessible
But without allowing them to overwhelm me

19. Brain to Heart

How do I get from my brain to my heart?

By listening to it
By refusing to ignore or dismiss its emotions
By allowing myself to feel
And to grant myself the time to explore the feelings and
emotions
my heart has
By making a rational decision to force thinking
to the background

20. Childhood Memories

20

She remembers the smell of coffee and tobacco
    on her grandfather's skin
She remembers opening the cutlery drawer and looking
under the tray for money
    to head out and buy food at the store
She remembers the tents her dad put together for her
and her siblings
    And her cousins and friends who came by
She remembers being afraid of going down the hall
    at night

21. Farewells

Saying goodbye is painful
There is no way around it
It hurts to know you won't see someone everyday
It hurts not knowing the exact date when you're going to
see them again
It hurts to let go from that final embrace
Knowing there might never be another one

After saying goodbye to friends
Your heart is never the same
A piece of is not with you anymore, but with them
And your only hope of feeling whole again
Is to meet somewhere, sometime,
And to reminiscence about those beautiful moments
That molded your heart and made it grow bigger
Than you ever thought possible.

Saying goodby is painful
But also hopeful
It gives you something to look forward to, and
The thrill of anticipating the next embrace,
Could be almost as exciting
As the embrace itself

www.ingramcontent.com/pod-product-compliance
Lightning Source LLC
LaVergne TN
LVHW021344200726
843509LV00014B/2661